It Rings a Bell

It Rings a Bell

STEVE M. SKUPIEN

Copyright © 2016 by Steve M. Skupien
theymovedthemoon@gmail.com

Mill City Press, Inc.
2301 Lucien Wat #415
Maitland, FL 32751
866-381-2665
www.millcitypublishing.com

All rights reserved. No part of this publication may be reproduced, stored in a retrieval system, or transmitted, in any form or by any means, electronic, mechanical, photocopying, recording, or otherwise, without the prior written permission of the author.

ISBN-13: 978-1-63505-410-1
LCCN: 2016913852

Typeset by: Jim Arneson

Printed in the United States of America

Image Credits:
Cover: © Biehler Michael
Page 5: © maodoltee
Page 15: © KUCO
Page 34: © Andrey Armyagov
Page 48: © TwilightArtPictures
Page 71: © Markus Gunn
Back Cover: © Bruce Rolff

"Publishing a book of poetry is like dropping a rose petal down the Grand Canyon and waiting for the echo." —*Don Marquis*

"There are . . . two kinds of spleen, one mocking, active, passionate, the other morose and wholly passive, when one's only wish is for silence and solitude and the oblivion of sleep. For anyone possessed by this latter kind, nothing has meaning; the destruction of a world would hardly move him. At such times I could wish the earth were a shell filled with gunpowder, to which I would put a match for my diversion." —*Hector Berlioz*

"To suppose that the eye with all its inimitable contrivances for adjusting the focus to different distances, for admitting different amounts of light, and for the correction of spherical and chromatic aberration, could have been formed by natural selection, seems, I confess, absurd in the highest degree." —*Charles Darwin*

"I am trying here to prevent anyone saying the really foolish thing that people often say about Him: I'm ready to accept Jesus as a great moral teacher, but I don't accept his claim to be God.

That is the one thing we must not say. A man who was merely a man and said the sort of things Jesus said would not be a great moral teacher. He would either be a lunatic—on the level with the man who says he is a poached egg—or else he would be the Devil of Hell. You must make your choice. Either this man was, and is, the Son of God, or else a madman or something worse. You can shut him up for a fool, you can spit at him and kill him as a demon, or you can fall at his feet and call him Lord and God, but let us not come with any patronizing nonsense about his being a great human teacher. He has not left that open to us. He did not intend to." —*C.S. Lewis*

CONTENTS

Such a Dish	1
The Blue Mask	2
The Forbidden Lake	4
What Happens to the Soul After We Die?	6
Marble Hats	7
Piñata (Batter Up!)	8
There're Crickets in My Casket	9
Darwin Was Wrong	10
A Study	11
You and What Army?	12
The Off Chance	13
If I Came Back as a Tree (A Lullaby in A Minor)	14
Not Unlike Pan	15
Gotta Avoid the Fires of Hell (A Campfire Song)	16
Christmas Morning (Grandpappy's Dead)	18
The Titmouse and the Church Mouse	19
Who Wants to Go to the Cemetery?	21
Did God Love Hitler?	22
The Thought	24
They're Running Out of Stars	25
Life's a Bitch	26
The Heart's a Home for Many Things	28
Lies (All Politicians Are Human Sewage)	29
The Eternity Train	30
The Colony Motel	31
The Soul Vents	32

Cooper's Terminal	33
Sick No More	35
The Tombstone Cutter	36
Gaunt and Haunted	37
Your Son's a Poet	38
30 Epistles	40
The Bumblebee Coat	48
Orion (A Jig)	49
The Retarded Professor	50
St. Lucy	54
Rudy Can't Fail	57
The Late, Great Kate Atkins	58
I Tried to Penetrate Her	60
Let's Start With the Sensitive Ones	61
I Want to Go to Jail	62
The French Quarter Ain't No Place for an Alcoholic	64
The Euthanasia Stop	65
The Despot: Revelation (A Dream)	67
I Can See Angels	70
I Remember You from Before the Womb	72
Services for Pluto	74
The Last Time I Saw Caroline	75
The Ghosts Inside the Attic	77
She Dug Her Own Grave	78
I'm a Holy Roller	80

Such a Dish

She's such a dish!
(My only wish.)
Better than any fowl or fish.
She's the T-bone on my platter;
The chickpeas, they chitter-chatter:
"She's so rare, she's so delicious."
This is where I got suspicious:
'Cause, the spud, I heard it say,
"I'd like to butter her someday."
(Know my wonton noodle wiggled
And the ghoulish goulash giggled.)

The apple pie I thought was tops
Betrayed me when it licked its chops.
My countenance, it had turned pallid;
I tugged the cloth, I tossed the salad.
It's true: I popped the wine—its cork.
I bent the spoon, I stole the fork.
Embarrassed now, I got a rash.
Rudely, I would dine and dash.
I had lost my appetite—
Went to bed hungry last night.
And now I'm glum, my spirits sag:
My dish is someone's doggie bag.

THE BLUE MASK

Now that you ask
About the Blue Mask,
I'll take you to task,
Now that you ask.

It's not nice to stare
At a face, unaware
Of what made it unfair.
It's not nice to stare.

Yet that's what you do:
You study the view
Of one unlike you.
That's what you do.

You've looked too long here.
You don't belong here.
You'll right the wrong here.
You've looked too long here.

What will you do now?
You've acquired the hue now.
Your mask, too, is blue now.
What will you do now?

Now it will haunt you,
Torture and taunt you,
Your uncle and aunt, too.
Now it will haunt you.

You'll learn to look through it.
I did, though I rue it,

I grew into it.
You'll learn to look through it.

You cannot remove it.
It ain't meant for the Louvre. It
Ain't art. You reprove it.
You cannot remove it.

The Forbidden Lake

The deep, Forbidden Lake is black.
All signs of life the lake does lack.
It's the Lake of the Suicides.
(Man makes his plans, but God decides.)

So how many hearts will have to break
Before they drain the Forbidden Lake?

Strange shapes gather there at the shore.
A goblin juggles bones, what's more,
The bones come from a finch. Ignore
The ramblings from the carnivore.

Weird birds watch those who lament and ache
'Round the rim of the Forbidden Lake.

There's a man who collects his tears,
He's done so for 100 years.
His solemn twin, he makes an oath:
"I vow to represent us both."

Two approach the shore, a track they make.
One returns from the Forbidden Lake.

On a rock, one's written verse. He
Makes it clear, it has no mercy:
"Waters, here, will always swallow
Hearts, hell-bent, both hard and hollow."

Will they drag the lake for heaven's sake?
Make more room in the Forbidden Lake?

I'm walking near the lake, I see
Its tongue engaged in blasphemy.
I call upon the one True God
Who'll help me (though austere) to trod

Past the throngs of those who can't awake
From their nightmares. The Forbidden Lake.

What Happens to the Soul After We Die?

There are those we despise,
There are those we make famous.
Good souls exit the eyes,
Bad souls via the anus.

Marble Hats

Birthdays come, the years, they mount.
Do not think that yours don't count.
You're too far from youth's fair fount.
Birthdays come, the years, they mount.

"I am thirsty," his mouth said.
"Death is sitting on the bed.
Dressed in black, its eyes are red.
I am thirsty," his mouth said.

Let us slip on the white gloves.
"Chitter-chitter": Nearby doves
Testify for our lost loves.
Let us slip on the white gloves.

Let us meet for lukewarm lunch.
Tears in both the tea and punch.
There'll be cake, I have a hunch.
Let us meet for lukewarm lunch.

Everybody gets a hole,
Like the ostrich or the mole.
Either cry, then, or console.
Everybody gets a hole.

Piñata (Batter Up!)

God spat into His hands,
Then positioned His crown.
He took a practice swing
With the rod, renowned.

Far off in the nosebleed seats,
Doubleday, he cheered.
Who would clean the Holy Cleats?
Gehrig volunteered.

A mighty swing! The rod had met
(It came in very handy)
The blue globe. Royally upset!
(The dead within: God's candy.)

There're Crickets in My Casket

There're crickets in my casket,
They play their violin legs.
They're aware: I'm a basket
Case. (They lay their eggs.)

How I love to hear them play
Their sweet songs, old and new!
I adjust my ascot, gray—
Tug the lace upon my shoe.

How I love this serenade!
How I love the score to this!
Now comes their nightly parade:
In and out each orifice.

(Musicians in the thicket!)
But who will marry us?—
Myself and the Queen Cricket?
Which Stradivarius?

There're crickets in my casket.
How, the lot, they groom me!
Oh, no! Here comes the maggot!
Worms start to consume me!

Darwin Was Wrong

There is a cure for death
And it comes in a pill.
Haven't seen it? You will,
But do not hold your breath.

You gotta be a Vanderbilt
To afford the thing.
It's promised to bring
Eternal life, by gum. The guilt

You may feel for living long?—
That's the price you pay, the glitch.
It ain't the FIT but the RICH
Who'll survive. Darwin was wrong.

A Study

They don't change.
By that, I mean the size
Of your eyes.
You're born with the same-size eyes
As one who lives long and dies.
Realize,
It may be odd or strange,
But the size of your eyes doesn't change.

Your nose and ears?—
That's a different story.
Through all your years,
Until old and hoary,
They grow.
So,
I suppose your ears and nose chose
To grow until your eyes close.

Look at any old man you meet
And don't deny they are replete
With these pronounced features
I've mentioned. (They're creatures!)

You and What Army?

You and what army
Can possibly disarm me?
I'm like Reagan and Rommel, too.
How I'd like to pummel you

With my arsenal of insults!
With my stockpile of slander!
I'll blacken your name,
Be it Al or Alexander.

What part of Mao Tse-tung
Don't you understand?
I'll Ceausescu your ass.
Call my hand.

"You and What Army?"
My calling card says.
No one can harm me,
I'm like Pol-Pot, Cortez.

The Off Chance

On the off chance we part,
And our love withers like Dali's
"Clock Art,"*
Should finale's
Fat woman sing
And we become undone,
Should the cord break which binds
Two into one,
Be used as a jump rope
By some poor boy,
Or as a whip by a lion tamer,
Or as a noose by some killjoy,
Let it be said that, indeed: We knew True Love—
That we were as blessed as any who knew love.

---

* See the painting *The Persistence of Memory* by Salvador Dali

If I Came Back as a Tree
(A Lullaby in A Minor)

If I came back as a tree,
I'd be tall and fit and free.

My limbs would stretch into the sky.
I'd be a host to things that fly.

Each branch of mine would be the best,
Upon which, I would offer rest.

What better place to sleep in me?
(I ask hypothetically.)

Know I would house the owl and hive.
The bee could buzz, the bird could thrive.

If I bore fruit while I did unfurl,
It would be food for the bug and squirrel.

My foundation?—my strong roots.
(Another of my attributes.)

More provisions would be made:
There'd be peace inside my shade.

Perhaps, more joy, myself could bring?—
To keep a nest, a nook, a swing.

And when I die, you must, you should,
Use my remains for firewood.

(My smoke may rise to skies above,
But you would feel the heat: my love.)

Not Unlike Pan

You can do better than me.
Even the ugly agree.
I've swept too much under the rug
And I've acquired every bug.

'Twas fun—atop the Ferris wheel.
'Twas fun—to see the clapping seal.
'Twas great—to watch the 'phant do tricks,
To pick the roses with the pricks.

But I am but a poorly built man,
Some strange animal, not unlike Pan.
(God of the wild, shepherd and flocks.
Known for the panic he concocts.

His parents: Zeus and Hybris.)
What I am saying is this
(Before I completely digress):
I'm a monster. A misfit/mess.

Gotta Avoid the Fires of Hell
(A Campfire Song)

Gotta avoid the fires of Hell.
Worms as big as your arms do dwell
Therein; fist-sized spiders as well.
Gotta avoid the fires of Hell.

As it was with the Holocaust,
The doomed have got themselves embossed.
The dying have their fingers crossed.
As it was with the Holocaust.

What's your take? Please share your story.
Do you believe in purgatory?
Is everything gonna be hunky-dory?
What's your take? Please share your story.

I think a few good beats remain
Inside a heart approved by Cain.
I'll turn it around, I maintain.
I think a few good beats remain.

And I know God, He prizes prayer.
(Are there enough to get me there?)
What's with the bird's nest in your hair?
And I know God, He prizes prayer.

Eternity's a long time, true.
But what on earth is there to do
For forever? I have no clue.
Eternity's a long time, true.

IT RINGS A BELL

I'm about to pass now, so,
If I can, I'll let you know
Where I am and where you'll go.
I'm about to pass now, so . . .

Christmas Morning (Grandpappy's Dead)

I

The hunters trace their treasures,
They're on the trail of the fox.
And man, with two hands, measures,
His journey to the box.

II

Let's put a pretty bow on yours
For all the world to see.
(Little Sally NEVER ignores
A gift beneath the tree.)

III

Grandpa's in his Sunday best,
There're coins upon his eyes.
(His two cents.) "At last, at rest,"
The vicar softly sighs.

IV

He was in pain, but now he'll rot.
(This great man did God's work.)
The body's cold, the tears are not,
And Sally goes berserk.

V

The sight: The girl is paralyzed!
She reels! (You catch my drift.)
She's not too young, she's realized
That death's sometimes a gift.

The Titmouse and the Church Mouse

Be well aware, this tale is tall.
"The titmouse ain't a mouse at all."
This I heard the church mouse call
From a hole inside the wall.

The titmouse said, the titmouse sighed,
The titmouse from the sky replied
(From a branch where it did perch),
To the mouse inside the church:

"I know you, there's no debating.
Here you go insinuating
That I'm some type of hypocrite—
'Mouse' in my name, yet, far from it."

"My name says *mouse*, but I'm a bird.
This is the fact you find absurd.
But consider this, I do insist:
Church ain't no place for an atheist."

The tables, they were turning, turned.
The pink ears of the mouse, they burned.
"You, mouse, you are the hypocrite—
Church in your name, yet, far from it."

"I have no faith; whom do I owe
This pleasure to? How did you know?
Who spilled the beans? Who's been talking?
Dawkins? Dennett? Harris? Hawking?"

"All of Mother Nature knows;
God knows too," the titmouse goes.

"You lack faith and therefore guts.
There are no ifs, ands, or buts."

"If you had guts, you'd take the cheese."
(The church mouse would the moment seize.
And though, indeed, its jaws might snap):
"I'll take the cheese, BIRD, from the trap!"

"I'll show you guts, you wait and see!"
The church mouse, incredulously:
"You put me on; you put on airs,
Believing in some man upstairs."

The titmouse from its perch it flew.
The challenge with the church mouse through.
The titmouse on its prey did peck.
The church mouse had a broken neck.

Who Wants to Go to the Cemetery?

Who wants to go to the cemetery?
We can dress up in sheets.
We could scare the shit out of everyone
Placing plastic flowers upon the graves.

Who wants to go to the old folks' home?
We can dress up as the Grim Reaper.
We could scare the shit out of everyone
Circling the drain.

Who wants to go to the day-care center?
We could dress up as the Bogey Man.
We could scare the shit out of the little ones
As they cough up peaches and cream.

Oh, I know it's odd to think such things,
But thoughts are birds and birds have wings.

Did God Love Hitler?

I

Did God love Hitler?
Is the Pope Catholic?
Do you know that a young Hitler
Considered becoming a priest?
True story.
Then he wanted to be an artist.
Did God love Hitler?
Does a bear shit in the woods?
Maybe if the Academy of Fine Arts, Vienna,
Hadn't rejected him TWICE
(Because of his "Unfitness for painting"),
He wouldn't have lost his marbles.
Did God love Hitler?
Do one-legged ducks swim in circles?

II

Then came the failed coup.
Then came the imprisonment
And the infamous manifesto.
Next, the wheels really came off.
The ovens came.
The Führer Furnaces.
(Satan had really got his hooks in him.)
Then, I think, God couldn't love him.
Then, I think, God wouldn't love him.
(I wonder if Hitler really loved Eva Braun.
I ask because the Good Book says:
"For love is of God;

And everyone that loveth is born of God,
And knoweth God."
If Hitler truly did love Eva,
I must assume that he knew God,
And yet he still cooked people.)
At any rate, Hitler took free will to a place
Where even the Creator Himself couldn't love him.

The Thought

The thought was bad.
The thought was mad
Because I wouldn't think it.
It kept ramming itself against my head
Like a moth bouncing off a lightbulb.

A lightbulb!
That gave me an idea
As to how to get rid of it:
This bad thought.
This mad thought.

(Although I almost thunk it,
I would have to debunk it.
Before it got into my blood,
I would nip it in the bud.)

I would drown myself on a whim.
Because thoughts like these cannot swim.
Think about it—it's my last wish:
Have you ever seen an insane fish?

The answer is no, 'cause such thoughts can't float.
They ain't like a cloud, a bubble, or boat.

They're Running Out of Stars

Ask Neptune, Saturn, or Mars.
They're running out of stars.
Some are named and some are anon.
Most of them have been wished upon.

The canopy says, "Enough's enough."
After all these years of wanting stuff,
After all these eons of wishing, wishing,
The bored North Star has hung a sign: "GONE FISHING."

(Don't get me started, you and them,
Upon the Star of Bethlehem.
The Three Kings had followed it.
Then some black hole swallowed it.)

The stars have crowned surfs and sages.
Every oaf through all the ages
Turning to the firmament for hope.
You're gonna need a stronger telescope

'Cause all the stars that you can plainly see
Have been wished upon incessantly.
They're OUT OF ORDER. (The naked
Eye can't see anything sacred.)

Don't you curl your lip or furl your brow.
Why wish upon dead things anyhow?

Who on earth beats dead horses?
Rely on different sources:

Wish in a well, break a bone,
But leave the poor stars alone.

Life's a Bitch

Everybody is black-and-blue
And not some kind of other hue.
We're all beaten up, through and through.
Everybody is black-and-blue.

I will admit that some are red
From getting kicked hard in the head
By Life, who's strong, fierce and well-fed.
I will admit that some are red.

Sleep—sometimes it softens the blow.
The world has not produced, I know,
One who can sleep forever, though.
Sleep—sometimes it softens the blow.

The man who puts up a fight loses.
He is the one with the most bruises.
Pick your battles, lengthen your fuses.
The man who puts up a fight loses.

Life's hard—don't antagonize it.
Life is tough—just realize it
Is brief. Nobody denies it:
Life's hard—don't antagonize it.

Why fight it? Put down your dukes.
Put away the gloves, you mooks.
All the uppercuts and hooks.
Why fight it? Put down your dukes.

Life ain't for the faint of heart.
Ravenous, it tears apart

Facsimiles and honest art.
Life ain't for the faint of heart.

Life is not unlike quicksand.
Let it run its course then and
Close your eyes and fold your hand.
Life is not unlike quicksand.

The Heart's a Home for Many Things

I

The heart's a home for many things—
Hawk or Dove.
Envy, strife, jealously, rage—
A house for Hate or Love.

II

Hers is the heart of the enemy,
Subterfuge and duplicity.
But know ancient Love will always defeat
This modern Hate (which prompts her heart to beat).

III

Her heart is gangrene,
A heart of rock,
Conceived on Halloween.
A twisted clock.

It's a filthy house:
It is full of fleas.
Inside there's a mouse-
Trap and rotted cheese.

IV

The heart's a home for many things—
Hawk or Dove.
Greed, malice, deceit, slander—
A house for Hate or Love.

Lies (All Politicians Are Human Sewage)

The White Lie
Said to the Whopper,
"I want to be like you."
And the Whopper
Said to the White Lie,
"You've got some growing to do."

So the White Lie visited
The brains of the twisted:
The pathological types
Who truth resisted.

What better place to go than the Senate and the House?
This is where the White Lie sucked from these hosts like a louse.
It studied their minds and took on the attributes
Of these sick fabricators inside their blue suits.

And this is how a White Lie trains
To get so large: to pick such brains.
(Know when the picking had been done,
Gigantic was the form it won.)

The Whopper said, "You've done all right, kid.
The envy of every arachnid.
The web that you've spun (to their chagrin)
Is larger than any spider could spin."

To hell with the politicians, their false promises,
Bullshit and ad libs!
(Know that the two Whoppers then ran away together
And had children: Fibs.)

The Eternity Train

There're a million cars upon this railroad track
And we're all going—
All the believers, to a place worth knowing.

Here's the thing: There's a car
For each one of us, ugly or pretty—
And everyone in between.
We're off to the Holy City.

"All aboard!" It's time to flee.
Throw your luggage in the sea.
The handsome folk get the Pullman cars
With windows by which to see the stars.

The plain people?—They get the coaches
Where you're served wine or beer,
Not bubbly, yellow champagne.
(You'll find me here
With my favorite hat.
Inside it: my cat.)

God Himself is tugging this long train
Toward eternity.
Let's light a votive.
He, alone, is the locomotive.

Oh! The homely! (Some would say UGLY)
Are bringing up the rear. Unsettling faces
Sip tea or coffee while the whistle wails:
"True Love Leaves No Traces."

God's got the devil locked away.
The war ends without a truce.
Satan howls forever inside the burning red caboose.

THE COLONY MOTEL

Here at the Colony Motel,
I wait for the front desk to call.
In the meantime, I shoot rubber bands
At the roaches on the wall.
A few limbs from the ceiling fan
Have been amputated.
I name each and every bedbug
That soldiers on, unabated.

There's blood on the carpet
Where something died—
A miscarriage or grape juice
Or a murder-suicide.
There's rain on the window
And snow on TV.
The documentary is poking fun
At Robert E. Lee.

I'm out of nicotine.
I lick the walls.
My tongue in the fly trap,
The front desk calls.
"Mr. Studebaker,
Your lady friend is here.
The one with the clubfoot
And broken brassiere."
But I'm sad, too sad.
"Please keep on your dress."
We nap and dream and sigh and smile.
We play chess.

The Soul Vents

I hate this house,
I hate this hair,
I hate this skin,
Thus, I'll prepare
To take my leave,
To take my rest,
To fly this coop,
This filthy nest.
This ugly cell
With bars of bone,
This belching body
Here on loan.
I hate the thud
Of this dull heart,
The dimwit brain,
Its so-called art.
I hate the ping
Of each new thought
That flits awhile,
But comes to naught.
I hate the sound
Of every breath.
Ye tainted dreg,
Inherit death!
(A dime a dozen, a flash in the pan,
Somebody please come and murder this man!)

Cooper's Terminal

Fate's a criminal.
Cooper's terminal.

"Divide and conquer"—
The battalion's answer.
The Blood Warlords.
The Contagion: Cancer.

Why are you so yellow?
Oh, I know now.
(At least have some Jell-O.)
I feel I owe now
Some prayer for healing.
Again, with feeling.

Fate's a criminal.
Cooper's terminal.

Your clothes are too big.
(How about some fruit?)
You're gonna need
A smaller suit.

Yet you'll live on,
If not through your organs, your pants.
We'll donate them to someone
Less advanced.

Fate's a criminal.
Cooper's terminal.

These are the last stages.
The army rages.
It's really uncanny:
It ain't satisfied 'til it's infiltrated
Every nook and cranny.

The victory is theirs! These rebellious cells
Raise a flag in his head.
His African grey parrot goes mad and yells:
"SQUAWK! Cooper is dead!"

Sick No More

Don't wanna be in bed again.
Don't want the Last Rites read again
Or have my fat fears fed again.
Don't wanna get sick no more.

I don't wanna, poetic, wax
Too much over the past, but facts
Are facts: There was too much Xanax.
Don't wanna get sick no more.

All the two-bit doctors tried to cure
The madness that made my mind impure.
(Their labor, fruitless; their passion, poor.)
Don't wanna get sick no more.

In due time, though,
Know

I learned God's assurance:
SUFFERING PRODUCES ENDURANCE.

The Word isn't mere literature:
ENDURANCE PRODUCES CHARACTER.

When I was at the end of my rope:
CHARACTER PRODUCES HOPE.

In the end, then, it was my mission
To understand this. The Great Physician
Gave me said HOPE. A new edition,
Ain't gonna get sick no more.

The Tombstone Cutter

I'm a tombstone cutter.
That's me.
I got a shop across from the cemetery.

I get paid by the letter.
(I've been saving.
I was cut out for engraving.

Come by and buy a slab of marble,
I'm here all week.
My clientele, in the ground,
Is primarily Greek.)

And with names like
MAVROKOUKOULOUS,
KARATHANASOPOULOUS,
And PAPAKONSTANTINDIS,
(There're many),
I make a pretty penny.

Gaunt and Haunted

Everybody is gaunt and haunted.
This is not what we wanted.
The people here are but black clouds,
Scudding, flitting, glutted with pain.
Then come the boxing glove–size tears:
Rain.

Whatever lives within a tear
Expires upon the carpet here.

I drank the wine, I ate the host;
Mistook the curtain for a ghost.
The thurible swings upon the hour;
Mistook the frankincense for a flower.
I saw a shape: the Candle Keeper;
Mistook the priest for the Grim Reaper.
I felt the breeze but did not hear it;
Mistook the wind for the Holy Spirit.

I'd like to report that there was some mirth.
After all, Aunt Bree had just given birth.
But the soft child cried, too.
A thorn in its side, too.
With eyes red and wide, too,
It howled, or it tried to.

Everybody is gaunt and haunted.
This is not what we wanted.

Your Son's a Poet

We heard the bad news.
It hurts, we know it.
It's all over the neighborhood:
Your son's a poet.

We knew something was amiss
When he washed his feet
With tears—crying for days
Over a dead bird in the street.

At least he takes care of your roses
And your periwinkles, blue.
(It is common knowledge:
He has no one to give them to.)

Dear, his heart's too big for its britches;
It doesn't know its own strength.
And those who wear their hearts on their sleeves
Suffer at length.

Does he have a death wish?—
He washes the hearses
At Flannigan's Funeral Home
Between writing verses.

We saw him on the roof last night
Speaking in rhyme.
(It was iambic pentameter
This time.)

Why he wore a cape,
A wig, and a mask,

IT RINGS A BELL

I'll be honest,
I was afraid to ask.

He was forlorn at the block party;
The rest of us were footloose.
He was counting backward
While he fumbled with a noose.

Sensitivity is one thing,
But you must know when to give it a rest.
It's over the top to tattoo
A bull's-eye on one's chest.

Our sincerest condolences—
I wouldn't wish this on my worst enemy.
And if you do not love him,
Know you're in good company.

Again, I'm really sorry.
I, too, have a son.
Know there is nothing
Anyone could have done.

Your son's a poet.
A stroke of bad luck. Could
You keep him inside your yard?
Sincerely, the Neighborhood.

30 Epistles

I

The suicidal cat
Went quite mad
'Cause its tail wasn't long enough
To hang itself.

II

He swallowed his wedding ring when they split
In the morning,
But they quickly reconciled
In the evening.
He reasoned that it would take a day or so
For the ring to pass,
So he took advantage of the absent hours—and absent ring—
And cheated on his wife.

III

I'm gonna return you—
Take you back.
Don't fret, they'll put you
Back on the rack,
And someone else will wear your ass as a hat.
Imagine that.

IV

I tried a blonde.
I tried a brunette.
I tried a redhead.

I tried a drag queen and a transvestite,
A homosexual and a hermaphrodite.
None stuck.
None took.
So I cloned myself and dated myself.
(Both our hearts beat in synchronicity.)
The only difference being where we part our hair.
Sure, he's much younger than I, BUT HE'S LEGAL.
We get along smashingly.
He has started finishing the sentences I start!

V

I got a tattoo on my face
Of my face.
Nobody can tell,
But I still feel trendy.

VI

It was dusk at the mental ward
And it looked like the grounds were filled with fireflies.
But it was just us nut jobs
Dancing around while sucking on cigarettes.

VII

0 is obese
1 is anorexic.
2 has scoliosis.
3 has an erection.
4 dons a dunce cap.

5 has a Frankensteinian forehead.
6 has a fat ass.
7 has a radical pompadour.
8 is wearing a corset.
9 has broadened its mind.
10 is Laurel and Hardy.

VIII

Straight from the bully pulpit,
I will name the culprit:
Chopra!
(And that eyesore Oprah.)

In fact, let's make a Capitalistic Sandwich,
Rich with fat, far from lean!
In between these two, let's slap
The meathead, Joel Osteen!

IX

All the suicide notes throughout all of history
Have been collected into one huge tome.
(It's not something you'd bring to the beach.)
It's required reading at the university
If you're majoring in Latin.

X

I wonder how many people
(Tru-la-la!)
Will begin serving their term
(Tru-la-loo!)

In Hell today.
(Hip, hip, hooray!)

XI

I don't have much experience under the belt,
But I want to find a girl who makes me feel like I felt
That time I found a fifty dollar bill
On the floor near the windowsill.

XII

"Mr. Peabody! Put your straitjacket back on!" I heard the nurse yelp. "How many times must I tell you not to refer to Mexicans as 'Piñata-Swatters' and women as 'Three-Holes'?!"

XIII

One of us left the other one;
I won't say which is which.
I ain't no stool pigeon;
I ain't no snitch.

XIV

Here at the Ace Bandage Factory, shrinkage has really
Decreased now that we've fired the mummy.

XV

I only need SIX friends remaining when I die.
(Every casket needs its pallbearers.)

XVI

"Poor Dreamt," said Dreamed, "Sucks to be you." (On being the only word in the English language ending in *mt*.)

XVII

Oh, sweet mercy! Oh, Dear God above!
The only person who doesn't love me is the person that I love!

XVIII

One grape to the raisin,
One grape to the wine.
One hop toward the herbal tea,
Another toward the stein.
One plumb for the pudding,
One plumb for the thumb.
One skin for the lampshade,
Another for the drum.

XIX

You burned my love letters,
But the only word that howled in agony in the flames
Was the word LOVE.
(My signature took it like a man.)

XX

My friend Renaldo is the roofer at the old folks' home.
He tends to see the saved spirits of the dead
Pass through the roof on their way to Heaven.

My friend Paco works the boiler room at the old folks' home.
He tends to see the condemned spirits of the dead
Pass through the floor on their way to Hell.

XXI

I can still remember my high school locker combination.
The numbers resembled my high school sweetheart's
Measurements: 18-18-18.
We all called her Olive Oyl.

XXII

She left me; you don't have to remind me.
At least I know that my worst day is behind me.

XXIII

One can never get an accurate sense of how one appears
Physically in the PRESENT,
Because one is always witnessing oneself in the PAST.
A portrait painter paints your younger self.
(You've aged upon its completion.)
Photographs—their contents—represent/exist in the past.
(A younger you.)
Selfies, same concept.

In the same vein, it takes at least a nanosecond for your
Reflection to rebound off a mirror and back into your eye
When you look into one.
Hence, you've aged SLIGHTLY by the time you've seen you.
CAN YOU DIG IT?!

XXIV

He was decapitated.
I had WARNED him not to play with his pogo stick
Upon the helipad!

XXV

The thumbs have revolted, and their resentment lingers.
They've left my hands because I didn't call them fingers.

XXVI

We went to the library and collected all the letters from all
The books
And made a big bowl of alphabet soup, myself and
The cooks.
(The vowels are sweet: A, E, I, O, U.
The consonants, they round out the stew.)
So stop by for lunch or consider it.
Especially if you're illiterate.

XXVII

Love and lust, they aim to please,
But nothing feels quite like a sneeze.

XXVIII

Today's the last day of April;
I'm gonna kill her.
May is my NEW love:
My Sweet Caterpillar!

XXIX

Did you hear about the balding bee?
He sported a honeycombover.

XXX

We had to jump-start his hearse back to life, which was
Funny because the defibrillator did not work on Grandpa.

The Bumblebee Coat

This one is for the books:
Hang their meat on wee hooks.
I have heard things about their knees.
I'm speaking of the bumblebees.
I thought—I think—a lot of her.
In turn, I'm thinking of their fur—
Fur from those who would buzz, flit, and float.
I'd make my love a bumblebee coat!
Fuzzy yellow, fuzzy black;
No sense of style shall she lack.
(I get a lot of ideas.) Please,
Help me hunt for the bumblebees!
Bumblebees to make the frock.
Do you have said bees in stock?
While I'm impressed by your bee beard,
The bumblebees, they must be sheared!
Now what about their meat on hooks?
Do you know any chefs or cooks?
Be aware: The beekeeper and I shall eat
The plump, tender, wee, warm bumblebee meat!

Orion (A Jig)

I tied a rope
Around the moon
And it was mine—
My own balloon.
I sang a song,
And on that note,
Me and my moon
Began to float.

(GLOCKENSPIEL SOLO)

Then came the god,
Not Norse or Mayan,
Rather, the Hunter:
Greek Orion.
I had wanted
A bird's-eye view
And I had one,
Until it flew—

(HURDY-GURDY SOLO)

His quick arrow.
It pierced my moon.
He brought me down.
He changed my tune.
I can't complain
(That's showbiz).
I have the earth,
The sky's his.

(36-MONTH-LONG DRUM SOLO)

The Retarded Professor

The Retarded Professor, he was hired
Because Dr. Foote was fired.
"He'd look up their skirts," said the nightly news.
(He wore mirrors on his shoes.)

The Retarded Professor has four eyes;
One would quickly realize:
One looked one way, the other, another.
(A trait shared with his mother.)

Because of this, the Professor could look—
Read both pages of a book
At the same time. He's a bibliophile.
(But he slept once in a while.)

The man knew Descartes and he knew Kant.
Part idiot, part savant.
Knew transcendental idealism.
The janitor would quiz him

About fate and art, about pride and bliss,
While he worked his abacus.
"Everyone is fighting a hard battle,"
He'd say. His teeth would rattle.

They were false and he kept them in a jar
When he dressed up as the czar
(Peter the Great). Practiced jurisprudence.
An ally of the students.

The Retarded Professor was aware
That he was losing his hair.

He didn't want to, but he kept it up.
(Rest assured, he swept it up.)

His glasses were thick, when the sunlight shone
Through the lenses, fire was prone
To break out and burn (sometimes flames would rage)
All our essays. Every page.

Let us get down to it, down to brass tacks
Before someone twists the facts:
He earned his title, had many degrees.
Often quoted Sophocles.

Sophocles—he of the Greek tragedy.
Author of *Antigone*.
(The great writer that the lit major quotes
Right before he sows his oats.)

Of course, most would say that Shakespeare is best.
The Professor would protest.
Realize that this was just his preference.
(William has earned due reverence.)

The Professor was as smart as a whip.
Told the truth, shot from the hip.
He had more on his mind than his paycheck.
He was prone to risk his neck

'Cause he cared for our SPIRTS and our HEARTS.
(Had a soft spot for the arts.)
He would bless us with sensitivity.
(That's something you rarely see.)

Taught history, science, mathematics.
Know he had his fanatics.

(In fact, I was one—you're allowed to laugh—
Who asked for his autograph.)

There were those who offered to iron his tie;
Keep the sun out of his eye.
Straighten his spine, shine his globe, clean his slate;
Help him chew the food he ate.

I'm honored: He took me under his wing.
I remember everything:
To take the road less traveled, just like Frost.
"All the others will be lost."

So said my mentor, my teacher, my boss.
(It was true: He'd hit the sauce.
But it has never been considered dumb
To nip the rye or sip the rum.

He was sober as a judge when he taught.)
All your knowledge is for naught
Because the Professor has more of it.
'Twas his take, the core of it:

"Anyone upon the Earth can be smart,
But it's wisdom that's an art.
Thus, acquire it and you will far outpace
Others in this human race."

"Wisdom trumps knowledge and it always will,"
He said near the windowsill.
A breath of fresh air he had introduced.
(From its den, his tongue was loosed):

"Imagination's more fierce than knowledge;
That you won't learn in college."

And: "Have faith in the things you cannot see.
God and love, especially."

And: "If you love only those who love you,
What credit to you is due?
For even killers love those who love them."
(Then came the cough and the phlegm):

These daring quotes caught his tow-the-line ear—
The Chancellor's. He'd appear
On the scene in his suit, his eyes would burn:
"Teachers teach and students learn!"

"No more of this out-of-the-box thinking!
Are you ill? Have you been drinking?
You are part of the chain here—a weak link!
At best, you're paid to make them think."

"Certainly you're not paid to make them FEEL!
You're a cog inside the wheel.
One by one, then, turn 'em out," he'd opine,
"Right down the assembly line!"

My dear Professor, he finished his drink.
Dipped the fountain pen in ink
And then wrote his resignation letter.
(Turned in his cap and sweater.)

He quit, and I wonder what he knows now.
Does he reap what he sows now?
My alma mater (and I do weep now!)—
They turn out only sheep now.

St. Lucy

I

I implore St. Lucy
To keep vigil over my eyes.
They are bad.

St. Lucy, the Patron Saint of the blind.
AKA, Lucia of Syracuse.
Her name means "light" and "lucid."
Lucid Lucy.

II

My grandfather went blind
Because some halfwit doctor
Gave him the wrong medicine,
Which paralyzed his eyes.
As a result, he was in darkness for decades.

God bless my grandmother
(Whom I don't remember),
Who stood with him through thick and thin!

They settled out of court
For one thousand dollars.
Highway robbery,
Even for 1940.

He should have been awarded millions of dollars.
A dollar for every scene he was made to miss.
As an heir, I would have helped anyone who had
TWO eyes but needed FOUR.

In short, if you couldn't see for shit,
I'd supply the glasses.
(I'd like to bring back the monocle!)
F.O.C.

I'd do it for Stevie.
I'd do it for Ray.
I'd do it for Helen.
But most of all, I'd do it for my grandfather
(Who still wore a hat,
Though blind as a bat).
He got ripped off.
He got the shaft:
A white stick.

III

LUCY!
Station sentries upon each eyelid
With swords drawn,
Prepared to ward off myopia!

YOU, reader, must say a prayer for me!
A novena for my eyes!

Now you're forced to say said novena
Because you're reading this stuff.
(Sucker!)

THE NOVENA PRAYER TO SAINT LUCY, PROTECTOR OF THE EYES

(It goes like this:)

O St. Lucy, you preferred to let your eyes be torn out instead of denying the faith and defiling your soul; and God, through an extraordinary miracle, replaced them with another pair of sound and perfect eyes to reward your virtue and faith, appointing you as the protector against eye diseases. I come to you for you to protect my eyesight and to heal the illness in my eyes.

O St. Lucy, preserve the light of my eyes so that I may see the beauties of creation, the glow of the sun, the color of the flowers and the smile of children.

Preserve also the eyes of my soul, the faith, through which I can know my God, understand His teachings, recognize His love for me, and never miss the road that leads me to where you, St. Lucy, can be found in the company of the angels and saints.

St. Lucy, protect my eyes and preserve my faith. Amen.

Thank you, Dear Lucy.
Thank you, Dear Reader.

Rudy Can't Fail

Rudy bought a gun when he turned 18.

Rudy was an only child who really didn't do much. He kinda phoned it in. Mowed the lawn occasionally, took out the trash, changed the toilet paper rolls. Never drew much interest from the ladies. He was 40 and lived with his parents. He was oily. To top it off, he had red hair.

He had a part-time job at the pet store and spent what he made on beer and magazines.

Now, one day it came to pass; or rather, THEY did: His folks. They'd been married for many decades.

You know the routine: When one spouse very old dies, the other is quick to follow. Shirl went first. Then Marty. They were ripe.

Rudy made off with quite a haul. (Marty had made a pretty penny in penny stocks.) Rudy would be set for life.

(The inheritance was in the high six figures, I hear.)

But Rudy was an asshole.

Their bodies weren't even cold when he took the six figures to the casino and confidently placed it ALL on green double zero. And when his number didn't come up, Rudy pulled out the 22-year-old .22 from his waistband and blew his brains out all over the roulette table.

The End

The Late, Great Kate Atkins

The Late, Great Kate Atkins kept her heart in her mouth,
Her blood in a bucket in a bank down South.
The fluids inside her, they splashed on my face
After I tossed her down the spiral staircase.
The thumping that followed resembled a drum roll,
And there at the bottom, Kate gave up her soul.

The Late, Great Kate Atkins: Her eyes, I stole.
Her discarded skin, I ran up the flagpole.
Her teeth were a necklace, her tongue was a rug.
Her spine, a walking stick, her skull: a jug.
Her colon, a jump rope, her scalp: a hat.
Her kneecaps were teacups; a trampoline: her fat.

The Late, Great Kate Atkins was a wonderful kid,
But she couldn't stop doing the things that she did.
Now who should be punished—the few or the many?
The righteous, of course, but there weren't any.
They held a quick service—the sensitive ones,
Who promoted the peace yet still carried guns.

The Late, Great Kate Atkins wasn't religious,
But her aura was godly, her beauty, prodigious.
The judge would now issue what I had coming,
But I knew there was a glitch when his fingers kept drumming.
He said with his gavel, he said with a thud,
"We'll let this one slide due to the lack of the blood."

The Late, Great Kate Atkins: She will be remembered
More for her stick-to-itiveness than for being dismembered.

Keep the faith and the peace lest you take the same ride
As the Late, Great Kate Atkins, who, as I've said, died.
I'm some kind of magician; abracadabra, presto.
That's my deposition. Heed my manifesto.

I Tried to Penetrate Her

I tried to penetrate her
Heart with a whisper.
I tried to penetrate her
Heart with a word.
I tried to penetrate her
Heart with a wish.
I tried to penetrate her
Heart with a sword.
I tried to penetrate her
Heart with a jackhammer, a time bomb,
And an intercontinental ballistic missile.
Then I pulled out the BIG guns
And tried to penetrate her
Heart with LOVE.

To no avail,
But I knew I'd fail.
(She DID get nervous, though; she DID change the locks
On her heart (always fortified like Fort Knox).)

"So why did you try to infiltrate it, you dumb kid?"

"Just to prove it impenetrable, and that I did."

LET'S START WITH THE SENSITIVE ONES

The alarm will sound if your heart is pressed.
Your kid-glove take is gonna be addressed.
It's your own fault, you shouldn't have confessed.
Let's start with the sensitive ones.

We must get you inside the gilded cage
With the rest of the runts. It's all the rage
To commit the sin and not pay its wage.
Let's start with the sensitive ones.

Now you look at the sky with a keener eye,
But you cannot compete with what rules the sky.
How can you be so calm with the ending nigh?
Let's start with the sensitive ones.

Who was that gentleman that you were kissing?
Why were you born with one skin layer missing?
Every nerve is exposed; alive, they're hissing.
Let's start with the sensitive ones.

You'd never withstand the future that's colder
Than ice or any stare or any shoulder.
By the time you read this, you'll be slightly older.
Let's start with the sensitive ones.

Some shed their pride and tears, others are trying
To gather their wits. Gravity's supplying
This death that the trap door had been denying.
Let's start with the sensitive ones.

I Want to Go to Jail

I want to go to jail,
But that's just me.
If I got any mail,
I'd build a tree.
I'd press the ink
Right next to my skin.
A tattoo, I think,
Would help me fit in.

(And the convicts would sing:
"Jail, jail.
Pay my bail.
Reverse the charges,
Forward my mail.")

I want to be framed
Or wrongly convicted.
I want to be blamed.
(My freedom, restricted.)
I'll kill or I'll steal.
(The D.A. indicts.)
I'd want my last meal.
I'd want my Last Rites.

(And the prisoners would sing:
"Jail, jail.
Pay my bail.
The gruel is cold,
The bread is stale.")

I don't want to be free
If I can't have you.
Incarcerate me;
I want you to.
I don't want to see you
With another.
Throw away the key, too.
Tell my mother.

(And the inmates would sing:
"Jail, jail.
Pay my bail.
I plead my case;
My appeals fail.")

The French Quarter Ain't No Place for an Alcoholic

The French Quarter ain't no place for an alcoholic.
Bourbon Street ain't no place for an alcoholic.
Pat O'Brien's ain't no place for an alcoholic.

"Just this one," he reasoned.
"I've been good." He seasoned
His gumbo.
Then more mumbo-jumbo:
"I'll just have a few
Then go home.
What they say is true:
'When in Rome!'"

He hit up all the joints:
HAIR OF THE DOG and TAIL OF THE DRAGON.
"The brain, the ale anoints!"
He fell off the wagon.

And then he turned into a monster
And puked.
He was compelled to call his sponsor.
Rebuked,
He drove his rental car in the driving rain
Straight into Lake Pontchartrain.

The Euthanasia Stop

Feeling low? Pills don't work?
Brokenhearted over some dumb jerk?
Hounded by your halfwit boss?
Wife prove to be an albatross?
Grown tired of the therapy
That just unearths more misery?
Are nagging aches caught in your craw?
Troubled by your mother-in-law?
Terminal? Do you have cancer?
Now there is a simple answer!

Here at the EUTHANASIA STOP,
We take away ALL of your ills!

NO fuss. NO muss.
NO questions asked.
(We specialize in discretion.)

Just choose a current periodical or a film.
Select one of our relaxing chambers.
Choose the flavor of your fumes.
THAT'S IT!
IT'S THAT EASY!

Why put up with life's pains?
When interest in it wanes,
Visit THE EUTHANASIA STOP.

"WHERE MISERIES CEASE
AND YOU FIND PEACE."

$2,000 per person.
$3,000 per couple.
$5,000 on holidays. (Open on Christmas.)

(Those under 18 years of age must be accompanied by an adult.)

Why wait?! Call 1-888-ALL-DONE TODAY!

The Despot: Revelation (A Dream)

I

The ashes of those who had burned
Were, by the Despot, snorted.
"The worm inside the imp has turned,"
The maniac reported.

The rats had a field day;
Each rat swallowed its tail.
And those who were sealed, they
Jacob's Ladder scaled.

II

The water was Bible-black—it was blood—
(It was heresy to say so).
The last scent that balanced atop the bud
Vanished. His horsefly halo

Circled around an ill-formed head.
(The flies fine-tuned their drone.)
The Despot denied meat; instead,
He gnawed upon the bone.

III

The full moon fell from the sky
And shattered like glass.
And those who did qualify,
Got the gas.

IV

The Despot chortles;
He swallows his food.
And the mere mortals,
The multitude,

Become a statistic.
(See what Stalin said.)
To be more specific,
We joined the dead.

V

Then the mantel melted
And the hot skin stuck
To bone: The bodies belted
In the back of the truck.

VI

All the seals were broken
And they came to pass:
The prophecies spoken
At the Midnight Mass.

VII

The river changed its course, then
Went dry.
And the Apocalyptic Horsemen
Came by:

Pestilence, War, Famine, Death—
Flanked by flames.

Each huge horse, with hot breath,
Quoted King James.

VIII

And Babylon's Whore, her
Dress fell.
(He, she bore.) Her
Home, in Hell,

Cracked open and the devil's
Kin swarmed near the cloven-hoofed feet
Of the Despot who levels
Foe, flesh, city, steel, and concrete.

I Can See Angels

They dart to and fro in front of my eyes.
They do not have wings, they are in disguise.
They'll visit both the foolish and the wise.
I can see angels.

They're circular, bulb-like; they're bright; they're fast.
They ain't the images of those who've passed.
They were created before time. Aghast,
I can see angels.

They do not have names, they do not need to.
They are sweet—they keep me up to speed, too:
Tell me Good News and what books to read, too.
I can see angels.

Surely, they care not for philosophy:
The overthink that mocks simplicity.
The simple fact is rudimentary:
I can see angels.

Yes, it's some kind of special covenant.
You can bet the farm: They are heaven-sent.
They're true to their word and benevolent.
I can see angels.

I wonder why on earth they'd look at me.
Once, an angel its fist it shook at me.
(It proceeded to throw the Good Book at me.)
I can see angels.

She said, "Sweet boy, you must stop with the sinning.
Know that we all backed you from the beginning."
Though the prince of this world appears to be winning,
I can see angels.

I Remember You from Before the Womb

I

I remember you from before the womb.
We were waiting for our respective mothers
Inside the Grand Hall inside Heaven,
Where souls await their marching orders.

We were but colorful mists then,
That hovered near the ceiling of the Hall,
Joyfully shifting north and south,
Just like bait in a fish's mouth.

You cried, too, when your number was called.
You cried, too, when you had to leave Paradise.
You cried, too, when you came into the world,
Where something isn't considered a miracle
(Birth) if it happens every day.

II

Life was good and not good.
Fair and unfair.
Fun and foul.
How was life to you?
We kept the faith.

Funny seeing your husk in hospice.
Now you and I are about to be called home.
We will reunite with our mothers, rest assured.
(They were great women.)
Perhaps I shall see you again in the Grand Hall
Hovering near the ceiling.

We could catch up.
We could give a few pointers
To the whippersnappers
Waiting to be born.
Waiting for their respective mothers.
Waiting for their marching orders.

Services for Pluto

My thoughts and prayers are with Pluto,
For Pluto is considered a planet no more.
Neptune's neighbor has been notified
And poor little Pluto is shown the door.

Pluto has been demoted to dwarf status,
And while the remaining planets have protested,
The brainiacs upon the earth have spoken—
The judge has rested.

My thoughts and prayers are with Pluto!
Yours should be too, dear Earthling.
In a gesture that warms the cockles of the heart,
Saturn gave Pluto a ring.

Pluto! It takes its moons with it:
Charon, Hydra, and Nix.
Also in the suitcase:
Kerberos and Styx.

Now I hear that its moons have been taken into
Protective custody
And that Pluto is on suicide watch.
(What a clusterfuck!) This is nothing less than
A humiliating kick in the cosmic crotch!

THE LAST TIME I SAW CAROLINE

The last time I saw Caroline,
There was vanilla on her lips.
Her teeth were as straight as ever
And it was warm between her hips.
Her blood, it pulsed relentlessly
Toward her toes and fingertips.
I was hers and she was mine:
The last time I saw Caroline.

The last time I saw Caroline,
She could have passed for a queen.
Her bones, they were gold-plated,
Every sinew, in between,
Was spun from the finest fabric
That anyone had ever seen.
I was hers and she was mine:
The last time I saw Caroline.

The last time I saw Caroline,
I thought that we would marry.
The best man was selected
As was the ring he'd carry.
But we'd never breech the threshold
We made imaginary.
I was hers and she was mine:
The last time I saw Caroline.

The last time I saw Caroline:
The last time that I had a spine.

I had tried to put my foot down,
But it was as if by design:
A murderer I'd never met
Rubbed my doomed heart in iodine.
I was hers and she was mine:
The last time I saw Caroline.

The Ghosts Inside the Attic

In the attic there are memories that sit there and brood,
Half-alive inside the darkness and the sad solitude.
Each one of them half-insane; "We are dying," they conclude.
Their hosts give them no static:
The ghosts inside the attic.

There is a dead clown with a white face that has given up.
There is a crack that keeps on forming upon the teacup.
In the corner: A lone mouse, on a raindrop, it does sup.
Their hosts give them no static:
The ghosts inside the attic.

In the web there's a spider who gets fatter by the minute.
Soon it will explode from all the dust mites that turn within it.
I feel sad for the insect; its eulogy, I begin it.
Their hosts give them no static:
The ghosts inside the attic.

The puppet inside the chest doesn't come out too often.
Broken with its heartache, it considers it his coffin.
Saturated with my tears, its outlook seems to soften.
Their hosts give them no static:
The ghosts inside the attic.

Ghosts throw no shadows upon a wooden floor.
Mouths agape, the shapes will groan forevermore.
Their lack of salvation leaves them sick and sore.
Their hosts give them no static:
The ghosts inside the attic.

She Dug Her Own Grave

She dug her own grave
And then slipped in.
The earth upon her,
Let the weed begin
To grow from a heart
I couldn't win.
Let a white flag wave:
She dug her own grave.

She dug her own grave
While I did sip
The morning dew
And mint julep.
My parting gift:
A white tulip.
Let the raven rave:
She dug her own grave.

She dug her own grave.
She used a spoon.
To make matters worse:
She'll rise soon.
Just like the heat,
My hopes or the moon.
Your tears, save:
She dug her own grave.

She dug her own grave.
One can in a pinch.

A cough, a wheeze,
I feel her flinch.
She's crawling closer,
Inch by inch.
The ground, it gave:
She dug her own grave.

I'm a Holy Roller

That's sufficient; it's time to go,
To put to death the status quo.
It's time to prove what faith does know.
I'm a Holy Roller.

All the sights I've seen are strange here:
Each buffalo on the range here
(And antelope) start to change here.
I'm a Holy Roller.

What do you make of the hole in the sky?
The trumpet call and the clarion cry?
What about the vision aimed at your eye?
I'm a Holy Roller.

Here comes the King; He will clean the clock
Of anyone formed from common stock.
Here comes His army, the entire flock.
I'm a Holy Roller.

I always knew it would end like this.
(It's all downhill after the first kiss.)
My name's written in the Book of Bliss!
I'm a Holy Roller.

www.ingramcontent.com/pod-product-compliance
Ingram Content Group UK Ltd.
Pitfield, Milton Keynes, MK11 3LW, UK
UKHW022235230426
12048UKWH00018BA/1277